GOING TO THE DENVER ZOO

Eric Parrish and
Ellen Sukovich Parrish

muddy boots

Essex, Connecticut

The first zoos

Zoos have been around for a long time. The first zoos were created more than 4,000 years ago in ancient Egypt and Mesopotamia (now known as the Middle East).

Modern zoos were created in the 1700s so scientists could study animals. Scientists and zookeepers kept wild animals in small enclosures so they could observe and learn about them.

Today's zoos give animals more space and create habitats that match their natural surroundings. These zoos not only teach and entertain visitors, they also study and protect the animals.

The first zoos were private collections of animals called *menageries*. Rulers and wealthy people kept menageries to show their power.

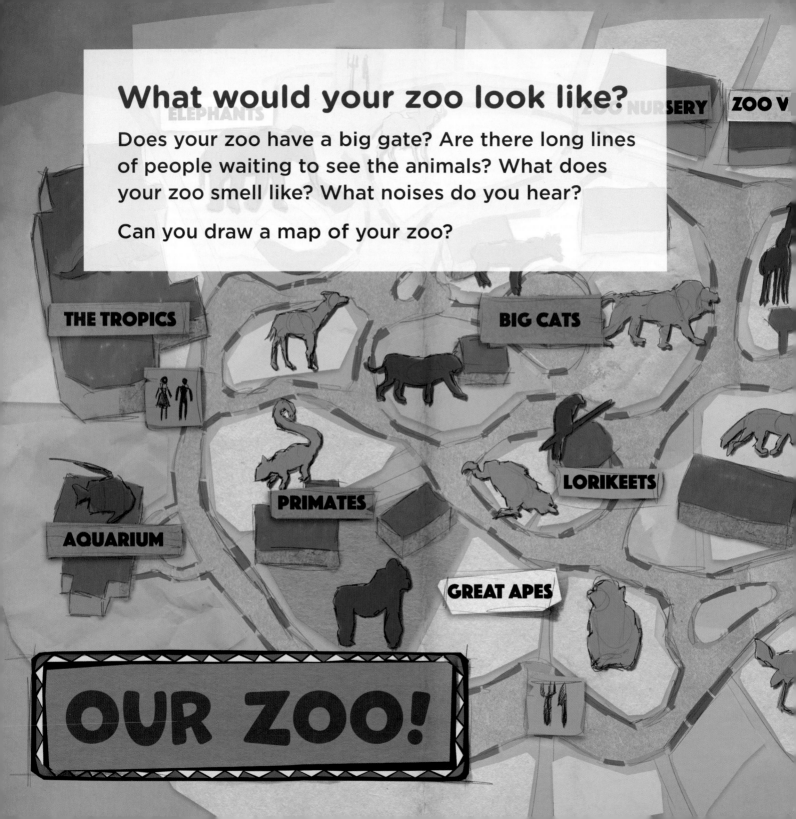

What would your zoo look like?

Does your zoo have a big gate? Are there long lines of people waiting to see the animals? What does your zoo smell like? What noises do you hear?

Can you draw a map of your zoo?

ELEPHANTS   ZOO NURSERY   ZOO V

THE TROPICS

BIG CATS

PRIMATES

LORIKEETS

AQUARIUM

GREAT APES

OUR ZOO!

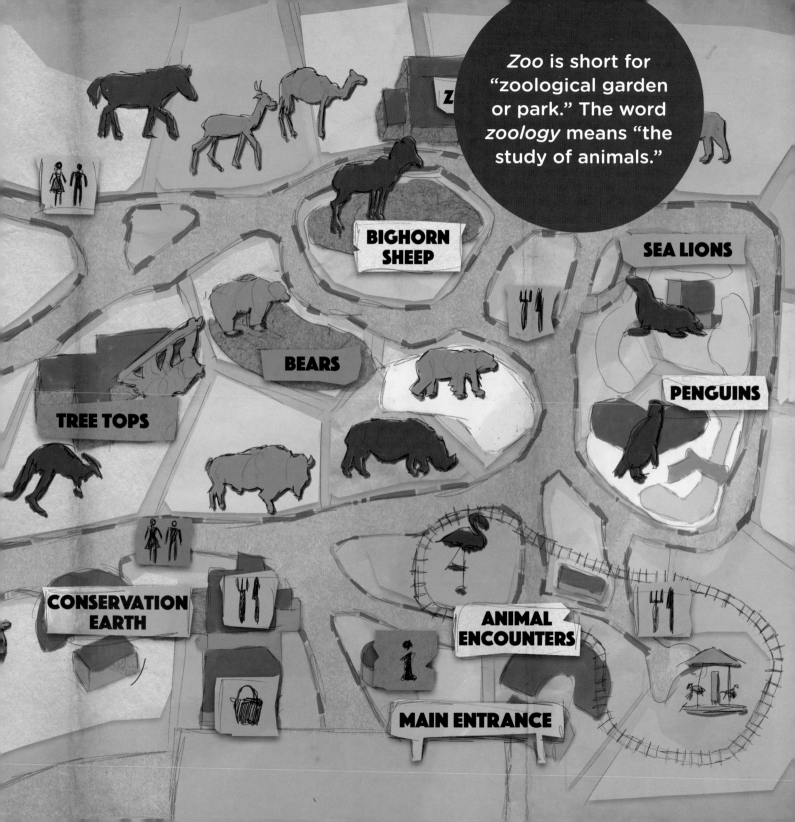

Zoo is short for "zoological garden or park." The word *zoology* means "the study of animals."

BIGHORN SHEEP

SEA LIONS

BEARS

PENGUINS

TREE TOPS

CONSERVATION EARTH

ANIMAL ENCOUNTERS

MAIN ENTRANCE

What kind of animals live at a zoo?

Zoos are home to many different animals. A zoo might have furry animals, such as lions and bears (mammals). You might see colorful flamingos (birds) or spiky lizards (reptiles). You might discover smooth and colorful frogs (amphibians). You could even see angelfish (fish) or creepy insects and spiders (arthropods).

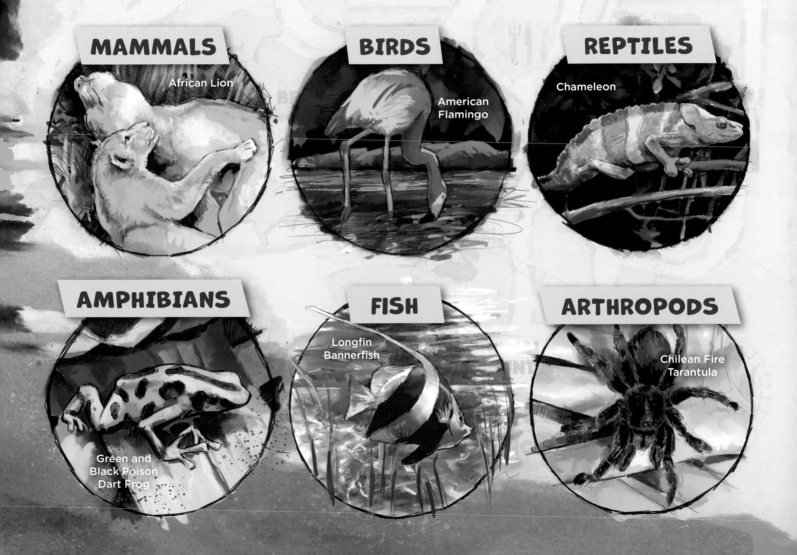

MAMMALS
African Lion

BIRDS
American Flamingo

REPTILES
Chameleon

AMPHIBIANS
Green and Black Poison Dart Frog

FISH
Longfin Bannerfish

ARTHROPODS
Chilean Fire Tarantula

FLYING
Aerial

Hawk

CLIMBING
Arboreal

Pale-Faced Saki

RUNNING
Cursorial

Cheetah

Blood Python

A snake moves back and forth in a motion called *lateral undulation*.

Locomotion is another word for *movement*.

Animals move in many ways to get from one place to another. Some animals have fins to swim. Some animals have powerful legs to run. Other animals have big claws to dig underground. Some animals can only hop or fly. Others climb and swing in trees.

Different animals move in different ways!

JUMPING

Saltatorial

Kangaroo

DIGGING

Fossorial

Mole

SWIMMING

Aquatic

Clown Fish

A kangaroo can move only its hind legs together and hop. It cannot walk or run.

African Penguin

Where do zoo animals live?

Each type of zoo animal needs a habitat designed just for its needs.

Cool pools for penguins to swim? Check. Tall trees for monkeys to swing? Check. A mountainside for bighorn sheep to climb? Check.

Many zoos create habitats with the animals' needs in mind. These habitats ensure each animal has space to move and comfortable areas to rest and feel safe.

A well-made zoo habitat will make it seem as if you are in the wild, peering unseen into the animals' environment.

PENGUIN

DIET: Fish, squid, crab, shrimp, krill

ADAPTATION: Penguins have hooked bills and backward-facing bristles on their tongues to keep slippery food from getting away.

HABITAT: Coastal areas on every continent in the southern hemisphere, from the tropical Galapagos Islands to Antarctica

FUN FACT: Emperor penguins are the biggest penguins at 4 feet tall. Little blue penguins are the smallest, standing only 1½ feet tall.

4 feet

I'm 7

Little Blue Penguin

Emperor Penguin

Sea lions can hold their breath underwater for 20 minutes.

California Sea Lion

Zookeepers are superheroes!

Zookeepers do everything for their animals. They feed, groom, and take care of them. They clean the animal habitats. They even pick up animal poop! Most important, zookeepers make sure the zoo animals are healthy.

To keep some of the animals happy and active, zookeepers "play" with them. They toss balls or play hide-and-seek with a toy.

This play is not only good for the animals, but it also builds trust between the animal and its zookeeper.

SEA LION

DIET: Squid, octopus, fish, clams

ADAPTATION: Although they can be awkward on land, sea lions are swift and graceful predators in the water.

LOCATION: Coastal regions from southeast Alaska to central Mexico

FUN FACT: Seals and sea lions belong to a *pinniped* (fin-footed) family. How can you tell the two apart? Sea lions have ears flaps; seals do not. Sea lions can also turn their fins forward and walk on land; seals cannot.

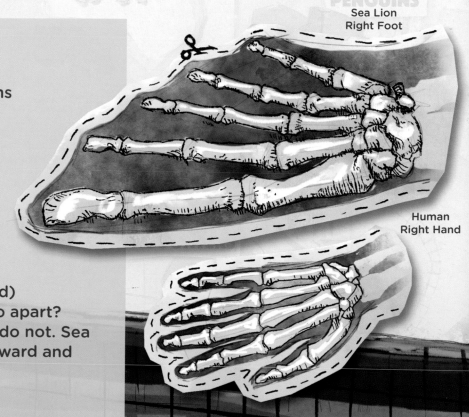

Sea Lion
Right Foot

Human
Right Hand

Rocky Mountain Bighorn Sheep

One elephant eats 200 to 600 pounds of food and drinks an entire bathtub full of water (50 gallons) every day. To get all of this food into their bellies, elephants must eat most of the day.

What do zoo animals eat?

Zookeepers feed their animals the same (or similar) foods that the animals would eat in the wild. They also try to feed the animals their foods in ways they would eat them in the wild. This makes the zoo animals happy and is good for their brains.

Plant eaters (*herbivores*) eat leaves, twigs, and tender shoots or "browse." Zookeepers give some zoo herbivores full branches. The herbivores then strip the bark off and munch on stems and leaves as they would in the wild.

Zookeepers give some meat eaters (*carnivores*) live, small prey, such as mice or insects, to "hunt" and eat.

BIGHORN SHEEP

DIET: Grasses, willow, sage, rabbit brush

ADAPTATION: With concave and flexible hooves, bighorn sheep can climb steep mountainsides with speed and agility.

HABITAT: Mountainous regions from the Canadian Rocky Mountains to the US Southwest and Mexico

FUN FACT: To establish dominance or compete for a mate, male bighorn sheep will race at each other and butt their heads. They do this with such force that the cracking horns can be heard up to a mile away.

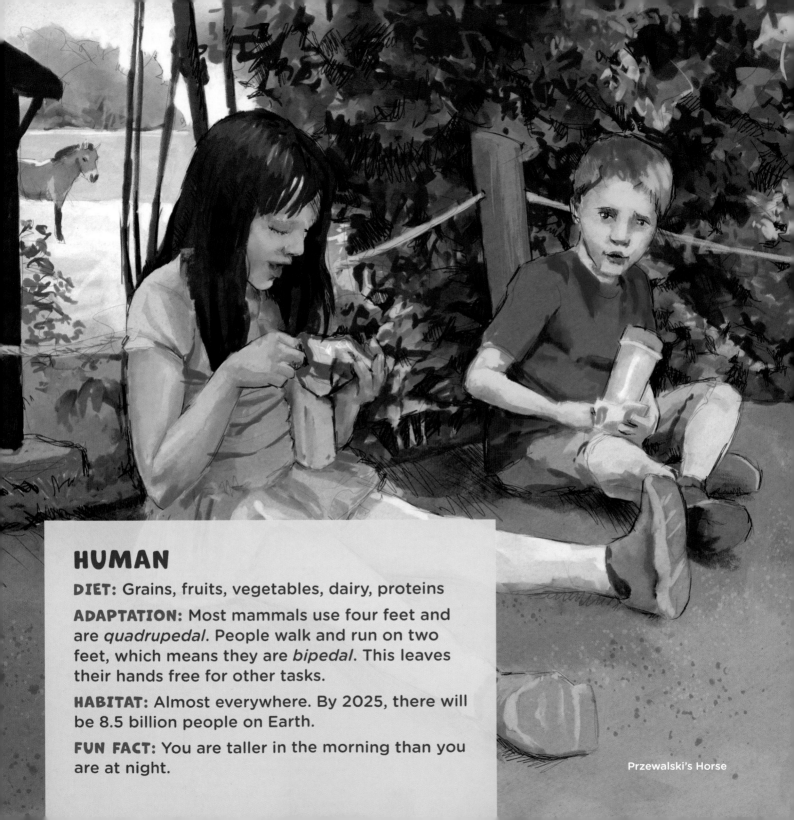

HUMAN

DIET: Grains, fruits, vegetables, dairy, proteins

ADAPTATION: Most mammals use four feet and are *quadrupedal*. People walk and run on two feet, which means they are *bipedal*. This leaves their hands free for other tasks.

HABITAT: Almost everywhere. By 2025, there will be 8.5 billion people on Earth.

FUN FACT: You are taller in the morning than you are at night.

Przewalski's Horse

Where does the food come from?

The zoo kitchen might look a lot like your kitchen at home!

The kitchen has big refrigerators to store food and plenty of counter space to prepare the animals' meals. You might see fruits and veggies in the kitchen, but you also might see branches, leaves, crickets, worms, and mice!

A zoo nutritionist carefully decides what each zoo animal should eat based on its diet in the wild. The nutritionist makes sure each zoo animal gets the nutrients it needs.

Why did the hyena go to the doctor? He was seeing spots!

Zoos have animal doctors called veterinary specialists.

These special veterinarians keep the zoo animals healthy.

Zoo doctors might check the bone-crunching teeth of a hyena for cavities or listen to a baby hippopotamus's heartbeat. They might help a mother sloth feed her baby or ease the aches of an old lioness.

HYENA

DIET: Wildebeest, zebra, gazelle

ADAPTATION: Hyenas have incredibly strong bites with large jaw muscles and sharp, extra-large crushing back teeth called *carnassials*.

HABITAT: Grasslands, savannas, woodlands, deserts, forests, and mountains in Africa

FUN FACT: Hyenas are not part of the dog or cat family. They belong to a family all their own called *Hyaenidae*.

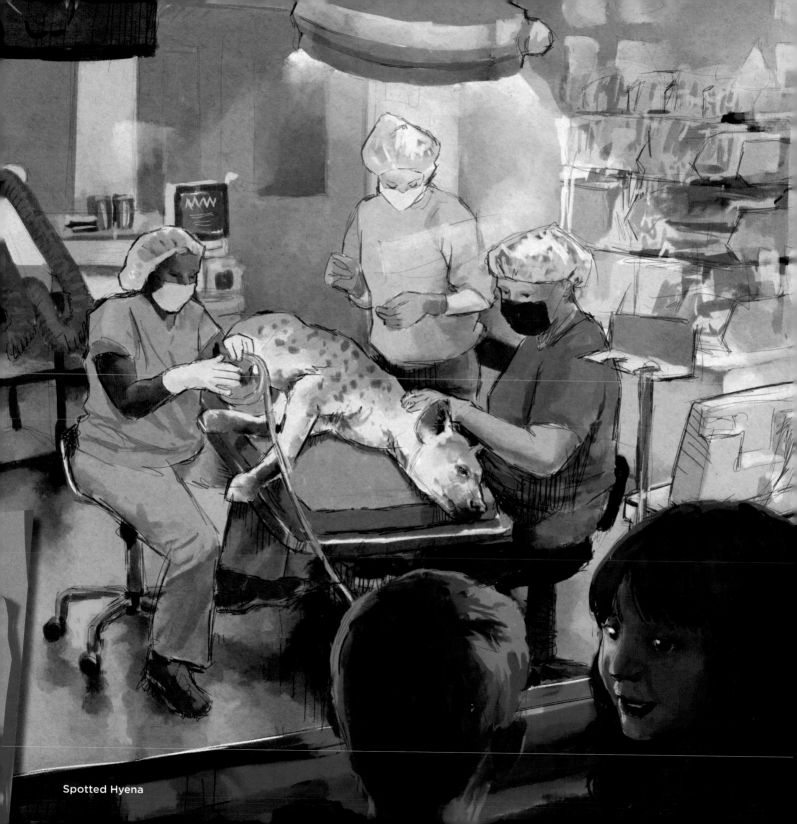

Spotted Hyena

Although scientists are not sure, dogs appear to have a common ancestor with the small South Asian wolf.

Watch this trick!

Zoo animals do not do tricks like those you might teach your pet dog. Instead, zoo animals learn trained behaviors.

A zookeeper might train an animal to help the zookeeper check the animal's health. For example, a zookeeper might train a rhinoceros to lift its foot so the zookeeper can check its feet.

To do this, zookeepers reward the animal with a special treat when it does the behavior. An elephant might get a crunchy apple for opening its mouth!

Border Collie

DOMESTIC DOG

DIET: Dog food—and sometimes shoes and homework

ADAPTATION: The domestic dog has an incredible sense of smell that is about a million times better than a human's.

HABITAT: Anywhere there are people

FUN FACT: Dogs were probably the first animals *domesticated* (tamed and then kept as pets or used on farms) by people.

Do zoo animals have to do tricks?

Zoo animals are not forced to do a trained behavior.

They do the behavior only if they want to. Sometimes you can see these trained behaviors at zoo bird shows or animal demonstrations.

Elephant trunks have more than 100,000 muscles, including sensitive "fingers" that can pick up small objects.

BIG CATS

ELEPHANT

DIET: Grasses, bushes, tree bark, twigs, roots, fruit

ADAPTATION: Elephants have giant back teeth (called *molars*) that constantly move forward like a conveyor belt as they wear out. Tusks are slow, ever-growing teeth—and that's the "tooth!"

HABITAT: Scrub and rain forests in Africa and Asia

FUN FACT: Elephants are extremely intelligent and have the largest brain size of all land animals. They are also very social and can express many feelings, including happiness, compassion, pain, and grief.

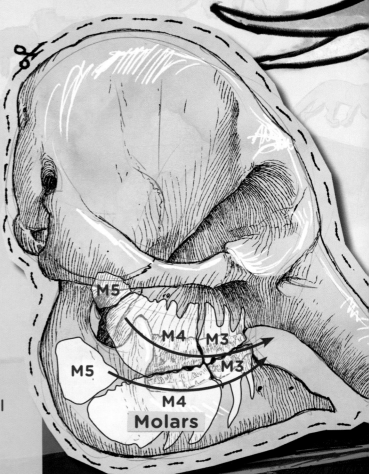

M5

M4 M3

M5 M3

M4
Molars

Elephants are not afraid of mice, but they are afraid of bees and ants.

Asian Elephant

Where do zoos get their animals?

Zoos rarely get their animals from the wild. Many animals found in zoos are hard to find in the wild because of overhunting and loss of their natural habitat. Instead, zoos work with other zoos to breed the animals they already have.

Some zoos create plans to protect animals in the wild. When we protect animals in the wild, it is called *preservation*.

When we protect the natural habitat of the animals in the wild, it is called *conservation*.

Captive breeding started with the domestication of animals more than 10,000 years ago. Early people domesticated dogs, goats, sheep, and chickens.

TIGER

DIET: Almost any animal, from chital deer to termites to elephant calves to rotting meat.

ADAPTATION: Large cats are the most specialized carnivores of all mammals. They have sharp dagger-like canines and knife-like cheek teeth called *carnassials*. They also have comb-like scraping *incisors* (teeth at the front of the mouth) used to strip fur and bones.

HABITAT: India, Nepal, Indonesia, and Russia

FUN FACT: The biggest of all the big cats is the Siberian tiger, which can weigh up to 700 pounds. Unlike other cats, tigers enjoy the water.

Only tigers, lions, leopards, and jaguars can roar.

Carnassial Teeth

Incisors

Canines

Amur (Siberian) Tiger

nectar

Lorikeet

Can visitors touch the animals?

You should not touch zoo animals! However, some zoos have special areas where you can get up close to the animals.

Have you ever wanted to feed sweet nectar to a small colorful parrot? Have you ever wondered what the skin on a rhinoceros feels like? Or have you wanted to hand a giraffe a snack of browse?

With the help of a zookeeper, you can meet some of the animals and do these things.

papillae

LORIKEET

DIET: Fruit, nectar, seeds, pollen, insects

ADAPTATION: A species of parrot, lorikeets have highly specialized tongues covered with small bristles, like a hairbrush, called *papillae*.

HABITAT: Forests in Australia, Indonesia, and New Guinea

FUN FACT: Lorikeets feed on nectar and help spread pollen from flower to flower.

Your zoo

Many of today's zoos have fewer animal species, but they try to have bigger and more natural spaces for their animals to live.

Zoos work hard to make sure their animals are healthy and happy. Zoos work together to protect the animals in their care and in the wild.

Zoos also teach people the importance of taking care of animals and the Earth!

Visiting zoos is a great way to get up close with nature. Where else can you see the majesty of a lion, the hugeness of a polar bear, or the curiosity of a tapir?

ONLY AT THE ZOO!

Many zoos have programs that support conservation projects around the world.

GORILLA

DIET: Roots, plants, herbs, fruit, bamboo, tree bark

ADAPTATION: Apes belong to the group called *Hominidae*. This group includes orangutans, chimpanzees, bonobos (pygmy chimpanzees), gorillas, and humans. In all, there are seven species of apes, including humans, and they all have similar body structures! Monkeys are different from apes because monkeys have tails.

HABITAT: Lowland tropical rain forests of central Africa

FUN FACT: Gorillas are strong and big, more than six times stronger than a human man. A standing adult male gorilla can be 6 feet tall with an 8-foot reach from fingertip to fingertip.

Gorillas cannot swim, but sometimes they like to play with water.

Western Lowland Gorilla

Koalas eat only eucalyptus leaves, and they sleep up to 22 hours a day. Eucalyptus leaves are high in toxins. The toxins need more time to digest, so koalas use a lot of energy digesting their food.

Time for bed

The amount of sleep animals need depends on what they eat.

Herbivores eat plants, which do not provide much energy. This means that plant eaters need lots of food. For example, elephants and giraffes sleep only two to four hours a day. They spend the rest of their time searching for and eating food.

Carnivores eat meat, but hunting and chasing food take a lot of effort. This means that lions and tigers might be awake only four hours a day to conserve their energy.

Omnivores eat both plants and meat. Humans are omnivores. We sleep about eight hours a day.

So You Want to Be a Zookeeper

Domestic Cat

Acknowledgments

The authors thank the Denver Zoo for their assistance with this project, particularly Dave Johnson and Jake Kubie, and the Denver Museum of Nature & Science departments of Zoology and Photo Archives. We also thank Katie Howard, Susan Denton, Rebecca Loughlin, and Joseph Loughlin for their feedback. Finally, the authors express their gratitude to Alia Rentz and her family.

Note: The zoos represented in this book are part of the American Zoo and Aquarium Association (AZA). The AZA is an independent accrediting organization that regulates the zoo industry, requiring its member zoos to maintain the highest standards of physical and mental care for wildlife.

An imprint of Globe Pequot, the trade division of The Rowman & Littlefield Publishing Group, Inc.
4501 Forbes Blvd., Ste. 200
Lanham, MD 20706
www.rowman.com

MuddyBootsBooks.com

Distributed by NATIONAL BOOK NETWORK

British Library Cataloguing in Publication Information available

Library of Congress Cataloging-in-Publication Data

Names: Parrish, Eric, 1972- author. | Parrish, Ellen Sukovich, 1979- author.
Title: Going to the Denver Zoo / Eric Parrish and Ellen Sukovich Parrish.
Description: Essex, Connecticut : Muddy Boots, [2022]
Identifiers: LCCN 2022026884 | ISBN 9781493072033 (cloth)
Subjects: LCSH: Denver Zoo—Juvenile literature. | Zoo animals—Colorado—Denver—Juvenile literature.
Classification: LCC QL76.5.U62 D467 2022 | DDC 590.7378883—dc23/eng/20220614
LC record available at https://lccn.loc.gov/2022026884

Printed in Mumbai, India | August 2022